MY FIRST BILINGUAL
Little Readers

by Liza Charlesworth

For Guided
Reading Level

B

NEW YORK • TORONTO • LONDON • AUCKLAND • SYDNEY
MEXICO CITY • NEW DELHI • HONG KONG • BUENOS AIRES

Teaching
Resources

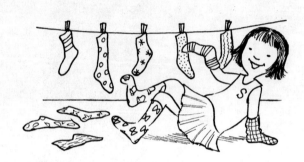

Cover design by Maria Lilja and Lillian Kohli
Interior design by Grafica and Ka-Yeon Kim
Cover and interior illustrations by Anne Kennedy
Spanish translation by Jorge Domínguez

ISBN-10: 0-439-02424-2
ISBN-13: 978-0-439-02424-2
Copyright © 2007 by Liza Charlesworth
Published by Scholastic Inc.
All rights reserved.
Printed in the U.S.A.

1 2 3 4 5 6 7 8 9 10   40   14 13 12 11 10 09 08 07

ontents

Introduction

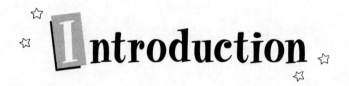

Welcome to *My First Bilingual Little Readers: Level B!* These 25 little books were written in English and Spanish to correlate with Guided Reading Level B. That means they're the perfect tools to support—and motivate—emergent readers with just a little experience under their belts. Research shows that offering children plenty of opportunities to read just-right titles boosts skills and confidence, thereby setting the stage for fluency. But what constitutes *just right*? Experts agree that a book is on level when children are able to understand most of the text. And when unknown words are encountered, children are able to decode the majority of them independently with the aid of familiar strategies.

Toward that end, the titles in this set were carefully designed to match the diverse needs of the many students you teach by presenting these age-appropriate characteristics:

* limited text on each page

* clear, high-support illustrations

* patterned text structure

* natural syntactic structures

* repeated and recognizable high-frequency words

* consistent print placement

* simple, familiar, engaging story lines

Although it's important for students to encounter texts at a variety of levels, reading too many easy books may inhibit kids from developing key literacy skills. And reading too many hard books often leads to feelings of frustration. However, reading a healthy number of just-right books provides children with a wealth of opportunities to be both challenged *and* successful. Via multiple experiences with on-level books, your students will be able to develop and "practice" a network of critical reading strategies including:

* predicting what will happen next in the story

* understanding characters and their motivations

* noticing the language patterns and style of the text

* figuring out unfamiliar words by using decoding skills to sound out words and context clues to confirm word meanings

* returning to the text to confirm understanding

* connecting the text to other stories and their own lives

* forming opinions about the books they read

With this essential skills set in place, children are empowered to ascend the reading ladder with increased agility, gradually mastering more difficult titles over time—until the sky's the limit! No, fluency doesn't happen instantly, but with systematic exposure to the right books, it does happen. And that's pretty magical. The *My First Bilingual Little Readers* series is here to help by providing a big boost to young learners during those all-important early years.

How to Make the Little Readers

Follow these steps to copy and put together the mini-books:

1 Remove the mini-book pages along the perforated lines. Make a double-sided copy on 8 ½- by 11-inch paper.

2 Cut the page in half along the solid line.

3 Place page 2 behind the title page.

4 Fold the pages in half along the dotted line. Check to be sure that the pages are in the proper order, and then staple them together along the book's spine.

NOTE: If you cannot make double-sided copies, you can photocopy single-sided copies of each page, cut apart the mini-book pages, and stack them together in order, with the title page on top. Staple the pages together along the left-hand side.

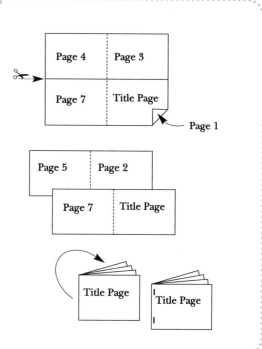

Quick Tips for Using
My First Bilingual Little Readers

Because *My First Bilingual Little Readers* are reproducible, they're the perfect books to use with guided-reading groups. Following are a few quick tips on how to structure your lessons.

• **Before Reading** Introduce the book, giving students a general idea of what the story is about. Then take a picture-walk through the story, inviting kids to make predictions and connect the illustrations to their own experiences. Encourage children to preview the text and find a few familiar and unfamiliar words. Discuss strategies children can use to decode unknown words, such as finding beginning or ending sounds, relying on their knowledge of word families, breaking the words into parts, or using picture cues to confirm word identification. Also, be sure to preview any concepts that may be new or challenging to children.

- **During Reading** Have students read the book softly to themselves as you listen in. Although children are reading independently, you are there to provide support and scaffolding. For example, you might guide kids to use word-solving strategies, such as "mining" on context clues, when they get stuck. Whenever possible, try to provide prompts and encouragement without interrupting the flow of children's reading.

- **After Reading** When children have finished, discuss the reading experience. What problems did they encounter? How did they solve them? You may want to return to parts of the story that were challenging, reinforcing word-solving strategies and discussing any unfamiliar concepts or vocabulary. This is also a good time to teach a mini-lesson on word analysis. For instance, children might manipulate magnetic letters on a board to unlock a word's structure. (For example, if there are several words in the story with short *-a* spelling patterns such as *-at* and *-an*, have children build and sort these words using their magnetic letters.) After that, you can invite children to reread the story and apply their new knowledge.

- **Assessment** There are a variety of effective tools to help you assess each child's progress. To analyze a student's decoding skills, take a running record as they read. To assess comprehension, invite that child to do an oral retelling. Additionally, it often makes sense to jot down some observational notes as children read, paying close attention to where their individual challenges lie and what strategies might require reinforcement. Armed with a deep understanding of every student's strengths and weakness, you will be able to customize effective teaching plans to meet their diverse needs.

Easy Ideas for Extending Learning

Following are some quick ways to use the 25 little readers as springboards to fun activities that boost skills in reading, writing, critical thinking, math, and more.

Growing Up • A crecer
(Life-Cycles Collaborative Book)

Create a collaborative class book patterned on *Growing Up*. Give each child a piece of paper, asking him or her to complete this sentence: "A (<u>baby animal</u>) grows into a (<u>adult animal</u>)." (For example, a student might choose to write "A joey grows into a kangaroo.") Have children illustrate their sentences. Then, add a cover and bind the pages together with O-rings for an engaging book kids can read all by themselves.

I Wish I Were a Bird • Quisiera ser un pájaro
(Dramatic Play)

Here's an instant way to shake out the sillies: Read the little book aloud slowly, encouraging students to use their imagination to pretend they are birds and pantomime each action of the story. Next, work together to brainstorm a list of cat, dog, giraffe, or elephant behaviors to act out in the same manner.

Tiny Things • Cosas pequeñitas
(Animals Sorts)

Build classifying skills by jotting on individual index cards the names of small and large animals such as *whale, elephant, rhino, mouse, frog,* and *butterfly*. (Hint: For younger students, you might want to include pictures clipped from magazines, too.) Now, challenge children to sort the cards into piles of big animals and small animals. Can kids think of any other sorting criteria?

Farm Twins · Los gemelos de la granja
(Twin Chart)

In this little book, twin cows say, "Moo, moo!" and twin pigs say, "Oink, oink!" What would other sets of animal twins say? Write a list on chart paper, then read it aloud together to boost fluency. Don't be afraid to get super-silly!

What Jumps? · ¿Qué salta?
(Internet Research Project)

Pose this question to children: What animal jumps the highest? A grasshopper, frog, rabbit, kangaroo, or dolphin? Then build Internet research skills by visiting child-friendly websites to locate the answer.

Gingerbread Boy · El muñeco de jengibre
(Listening-Skills Art Activity)

Sharpen listening skills by providing each student with a construction-paper gingerbread-boy template along with two eyes, one nose, one mouth, four buttons, two ears, and some glue. Now, read each page of the story, challenging children to listen carefully to your directions in order to create their very own gingerbread boys—just like those in the little book!

My Meatball · Mi albóndiga
(Sight-Word Game)

Here's an easy way to make sight-word knowledge whimsical and fun: Write 20 or so must-know sight words on index cards and place them in a pocket chart. Also, cut a red circle from construction paper to represent a meatball. Now, place the "meatball" beside one of the word cards, exclaiming, "Oh, no! What word did my meatball roll next to?" Invite students to shout out the answer. Then place the meatball beside all the other sight words in turn.

Animal Crackers · Galletitas de animales
(Vocabulary Box)

Build vocabulary and spelling skills by making your own flash cards, each featuring the name and picture of a different animal. Tuck them inside an empty box of animal crackers, then invite groups of children to "play" with the cards and invent their own games.

Ice Cream Scoops · Bolas de helado
(Ice Cream Estimation)

From flannel, cut a triangular cone shape plus several colorful circles to represent scoops of ice cream. Place these on your flannel board. Now, hone mental math skills by piling 10, 12, or 15 scoops on the cone. Invite a volunteer to quickly estimate the total. Ask a second volunteer to check the answer with an actual count. Repeat the activity several times with different numbers of scoops.

What Grows on Trees? · ¿Qué crece en los árboles?
(Fruit and Vegetable Sort)

Build classifying skills by jotting on individual index cards the names of fruits and vegetables such as *apple, pear, pineapple, lettuce, broccoli,* and *corn.* (Hint: For younger students, you might want to include pictures clipped from magazines, too.) Then, challenge children to sort the cards into piles of fruits and vegetables. Can kids think of any other sorting criteria?

Clean Up, Clean Up! · ¡A recoger, a recoger! (Clean-Up Chant)

Use this little book to help remind students to keep the classroom neat and tidy. With students, brainstorm a list of things kids can do to keep it clean such as "Clean up, clean up! We put our backpacks in the cubbies." Or "Clean up, clean up! We put our markers in the baskets." Recopy your favorite lines onto chart paper, then chant them together for fluency-building fun.

What Flies? · ¿Qué vuela? (Online Research)

Use this engaging book as the catalyst for a little online research. First, brainstorm a list of all the animals kids can think of that fly, such as a duck, a hummingbird, or even an extinct pterosaur. Then, demonstrate how to use a search engine to locate a child-friendly site to learn more about one—or more—of the creatures on their list.

Great Hair · Hermosas cabellos
(Diversity Bulletin Board)

Provide each child with a paper-doll template along with a variety of art supplies including yarn of varying textures and colors. Then, invite children to create mini-likenesses of themselves, paying close attention to their hair. Kids should also complete this sentence strip: "(Name) has (adjective) hair." (For example, a student might write, "Suzanne has red hair.") When the dolls are complete, affix them—along with the sentence strips—to a bulletin board titled *Great Hair.*

Come Over · Ven a verme
(Round-Robin Read-Aloud)

Copy the story onto chart paper. Then, fine-tune fluency by inviting groups of students to take turns reading each line round-robin style. If you like, innovate the text by adding some original sentences, such as "Come over and see my sink" or "Come over and see my rug."

Halloween (Costume Big Book)

Use this fun Halloween story as a model for creating a Costume Big Book. Pass out large sheets of oaktag, inviting each student to complete this sentence: "Here is a (type of costume)!" and add an illustration. (For example, a child might write and draw "a firefighter.") Bind the pages together with O-rings, then share the book at story time for a literacy-boosting read-aloud that's sure to capture kids' imaginations.

Party Shapes · Las figuras de la fiesta
(Shape Search)

Develop classification skills by holding up construction paper cutouts of each shape in the story (triangle, rectangle, square, circle, oval), then challenging children to look around the room to find objects that fit into each group. Which shape is the most prevalent? The least?

The Missing Monster · El monstruo desaparecido
(One-Minute Transition)

This quick transition is sure to reinforce your students' powers of observation and time-telling abilities. Craft a silly monster from construction paper (or ask a student to make one). Next, invite one child to leave the room as you hide the monster in plain sight, such as on a shelf or atop your gerbil cage. Can that student find the monster in one rotation of the minute hand or less? Repeat the activity throughout the day.

The Wheels on the Bus · Las ruedas del autobús
(Pairing Print and Pictures)

Copy on a sentence strip each line from this little book and place in your pocket chart. Also, prepare cards with simple drawings or photos of each vehicle type. When the prep is complete, build fluency by reading your chart together, challenging volunteers to come forward and match each vehicle type with the appropriate line. (For example, a child would place a picture of the fire engine beside the line, *The wheels on the fire engine go round and round.*)

Draw a Cat · Dibuja un gato
(Follow-the-Directions Art Activity)

After children have enjoyed this little book, develop their ability to follow directions by using it as a step-by-step guide to help kids draw their very own shape-cat—just like the one in the book!

Bigger · Más grande
(Flannel-Board Size Sequencing)

From flannel, cut these animal shapes roughly to scale: caterpillar, mouse, cat, dog, gorilla, bear, rhino, elephant, and blue whale. Now, place them in random order on a flannel board, challenging pairs of students to sequence them from smallest to biggest or biggest to smallest. Can children think of other sequencing ideas, such as ABC order?

What Do Monsters Eat? · ¿Qué comen los monstruos?
(Super-Silly Collaborative Book)

Create a collaborative class book patterned on *What Do Monsters Eat?* Give each child a piece of paper, asking him or her to complete this sentence: "Some monsters eat _____." (For example, a student might write "Some monsters eat bikes.") Have students illustrate their sentences. Then, add a cover and bind the pages together with O-rings for a super silly book that tickles the funny bone.

In My Pocket · En mi bolsillo
(Object Collaborative Book)

Create a collaborative class book patterned on *In My Pocket*. Give each child a piece of paper with a pocket-shaped page and this sentence to complete: "In my pocket I have a special [object]." (For example, a student might write, "In my pocket I have a special gumball.") Have students illustrate their sentences. Then, add a cover and bind the pages together with O-rings for an adorable send-home book parents will love.

Cloud Pictures · Nubes con formas
(Flannel-Board Cloud Shapes)

Reinforce kids' powers of observation—and creativity!—
by cutting white flannel "clouds" in the shapes of familiar
objects such as a bell, a snowman, or a tree. Place each on
your flannel board, challenging students to tell you what
the cloud shape looks like. Welcome creative responses.
For extra fun, invite students to cut out their own cloud
shapes to share with classmates.

I Like Socks · Me gustan las medias
(Clothesline Sock Show)

Pass out sock-shaped templates to each child with this
sentence to complete: "I like socks with _____."
Now, invite children to complete the sentence and illustrate
their socks accordingly. For example, a student might write
"I like socks with ice cream cones" and cover their template
with ice-cream cone shapes. When the projects are complete,
hang them on a classroom clothesline for everyone to enjoy.

Meet My Baby Brother · Te presento a mi hermanito
(Collaborative Big Book)

What are some other things that baby brothers, like Ray,
like to do? Work together with your students to make a list.
Then, use it to create your own big book patterned on *Meet
My Baby Brother*.

Growing Up

A crecer

3

A lamb grows into a sheep.

El corderito crece hasta llegar a ser un cordero.

My First Bilingual Little Readers • Level B

4

A puppy grows into a dog.

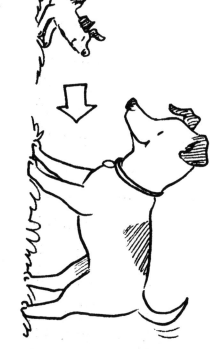

El cachorrito crece hasta llegar a ser un perro.

7

I will grow to be a very big man!

¡Yo creceré hasta llegar a ser un hombre muy grande!

1

A kitten grows into a cat.

El gatito crece hasta llegar a ser un gato.

2

A tadpole grows into a frog.

El renacuajo crece hasta llegar a ser una rana.

6

A piglet grows into a pig.

El cerdito crece hasta llegar a ser un cerdo.

5

A cub grows into a bear.

El osito crece hasta llegar a ser un oso.

Podría vivir en un nido.

I could live in a nest.

I Wish I Were a Bird

Quisiera ser un pájaro

Podría volar por todas partes.

I could fly all around.

I wish I were a cat.

Quisiera ser un gato.

1

I wish I were a bird.

Quisiera ser un pájaro.

2

I could hatch from an egg.

Podría nacer de un huevo.

5

I could eat a worm.

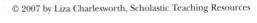

Podría comer una lombriz.

6

Yuck!

¡Uf!

Cosas pequeñitas

Tiny Things

3

There is a tiny ladybug.

Hay una mariquita pequeñita.

My First Bilingual Little Readers • Level B

© 2007 by Liza Charlesworth, Scholastic Teaching Resources

4

There is a tiny grasshopper.

Hay un grillo pequeñito.

There is a giant. It is me!

Hay una gigante. ¡Soy yo!

7

1

Look in the garden. What do you see?

Mira en el jardín.
¿Qué ves?

2

There is a tiny fly.

Hay una mosca pequeñita.

6

Hay una hormiga pequeñita.

There is a tiny ant.

5

There is a tiny bee.

Hay una abeja pequeñita.

Twin lambs say, "Baah, baah!"

¡Bee! ¡Bee!

Los corderitos gemelos dicen:
—¡Bee, bee!

My First Bilingual Little Readers • Level B

© 2007 by Liza Charlesworth, Scholastic Teaching Resources

Farm Twins

Los gemelos de la granja

Twin ducks say, "Quack, quack!"

¡Cuac! ¡Cuac!

Los patos gemelos dicen:
—¡Cuac, cuac!

Twin sisters say, "Hello, hello!"

¡Hola! ¡Hola!

Las hermanas gemelas dicen:
—¡Hola, hola!

1

Twin cows say, "Moo, moo!"

¡Muu! ¡Muu!

Las vacas gemelas dicen:
—¡Muu, muu!

My First Bilingual Little Readers • Level B

© 2007 by Liza Charlesworth, Scholastic Teaching Resources

2

Twin pigs say, "Oink, oink!"

¡Ruf! ¡Ruf!

Los cerdos gemelos dicen:
—¡Ruf, ruf!

6

Twin horses say, "Neigh, neigh!"

¡Nee! ¡Nee!

Los caballos gemelos dicen:
—¡Nee, nee!

5

Twin chicks say, "Peep, peep!"

¡Pío! ¡Pío!

Los pollitos gemelos dicen:
—¡Pío, pío!

¿Qué salta?

What Jumps?

3

A rabbit jumps.
Wow!

El conejo salta.
¡Huy!

My First Bilingual Little Readers • Level B

© 2007 by Liza Charlesworth, Scholastic Teaching Resources

4

A kangaroo jumps.
Wow!

El canguro salta.
¡Huy!

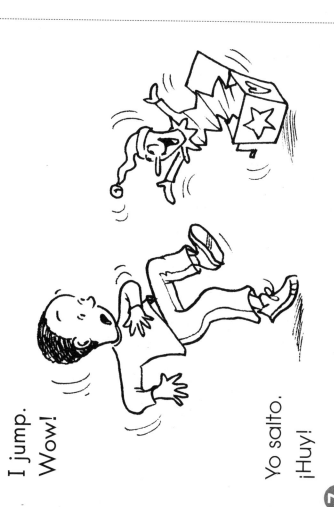

I jump.
Wow!

Yo salto.
¡Huy!

7

2

A frog jumps.
Wow!

La rana salta.
¡Huy!

1

A grasshopper jumps.
Wow!

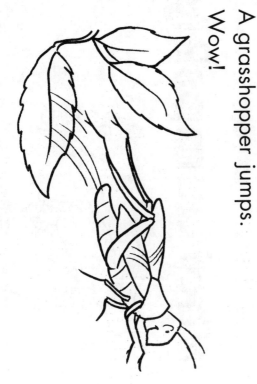

El grillo salta.
¡Huy!

My First Bilingual Little Readers • Level B

© 2007 by Liza Charlesworth, Scholastic Teaching Resources

5

A dolphin jumps.
Wow!

El delfín salta.
¡Huy!

6

A jack-in-the-box jumps.
Wow!

El muñeco salta.
¡Huy!

Then, I put on one nose.

Después, le pongo una nariz.

My First Bilingual Little Readers • Level B

© 2007 by Liza Charlesworth, Scholastic Teaching Resources

Gingerbread Boy

El muñeco de jengibre

Then, I put on one mouth.

Después, le pongo una boca.

Hey! Come back here!

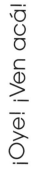

¡Oye! ¡Ven acá!

2

Primero, le pongo los dos ojos.

First, I put on two eyes.

1

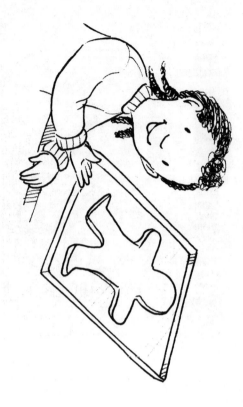

Let's make a gingerbread boy.

Vamos a hacer un muñeco de jengibre.

5

Después, le pongo cuatro botones.

Then, I put on four buttons.

6

Then, I put on two ears.

Después, le pongo dos orejas.

Oh, no!
It rolled past my book.

¡Oh, no!
Pasó por al lado de mi libro.

My Meatball

Mi albóndiga

My First Bilingual Little Readers • Level B

© 2007 by Liza Charlesworth, Scholastic Teaching Resources

Oh, no!
It rolled past my blocks.

¡Oh, no!
Pasó por al lado de mis cubos.

Oh, no!
Good-bye, meatball.

¡Oh, no!
Adiós, albóndiga.

1

Oh, no!
My meatball rolled off my plate.

¡Oh, no!
Mi albóndiga rodó fuera del plato.

2

Oh, no!
It rolled past my car.

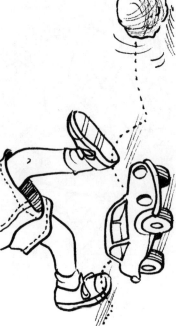
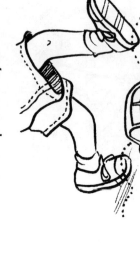

¡Oh, no!
Pasó por al lado de mi carro.

6

Oh, no!
It rolled past my cat.

¡Oh, no!
Pasó por al lado de mi gato.

5

Oh, no!
It rolled past my teddy bear.

¡Oh, no!
Pasó por al lado de mi osito.

Look at my bear.

Mira mi oso.

Look at my ape.

Mira mi mono.

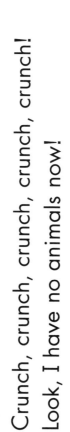

Animal Crackers

Galletitas de animales

Crunch, crunch, crunch, crunch, crunch!
Look, I have no animals now!

¡Crach, crach, crach, crach, crach!
Mira, ¡ahora ya no tengo animales!

¡Qué rico!

1

¿Quieres ver mis animales?

Want to look at my animals?

Galletitas de animales

My First Bilingual Little Readers • Level B

© 2007 by Liza Charlesworth, Scholastic Teaching Resources

2

Mira mi venado.

Look at my deer.

Galletitas de animales

5

Mira mi serpiente.

Look at my snake.

6

Mira mi vaca.

Look at my cow.

Galletitas de animales

Ice Cream Scoops

Bolas de helado

3

This cone has three scoops of ice cream.
May I have more, please?

Este barquillo tiene tres bolas de helado. ¿Me sirves más, por favor?

My First Bilingual Little Readers • Level B

© 2007 by Liza Charlesworth, Scholastic Teaching Resources

4

This cone has four scoops of ice cream.
May I have more, please?

Este barquillo tiene cuatro bolas de helado. ¿Me sirves más, por favor?

7

This cone has no scoops of ice cream.
May I have more, please?

Este barquillo no tiene bolas de helado. ¿Me sirves más, por favor?

1

This cone has one scoop of ice cream.
May I have more, please?

Este barquillo tiene una bola de
helado. ¿Me sirves más, por favor?

2

This cone has two scoops of ice cream.
May I have more, please?

Este barquillo tiene dos bolas de
helado. ¿Me sirves más, por favor?

5

This cone has five scoops of ice cream.
May I have more, please?

Este barquillo tiene cinco bolas de
helado. ¿Me sirves más, por favor?

6

Oh, no!

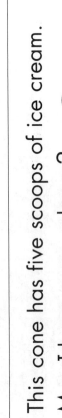

¡Oh, no!

Do peaches grow on trees?
Yes!

¿Crecen los melocotones en los árboles? ¡Sí!

What Grows on Trees?

¿Qué crece en los árboles?

My First Bilingual Little Readers • Level B

© 2007 by Liza Charlesworth, Scholastic Teaching Resources

Do pears grow on trees?
Yes!

¿Crecen las peras en los árboles? ¡Sí!

Do cupcakes grow on trees?
No! But if they did, it would be great.

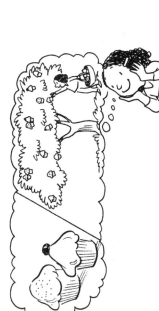
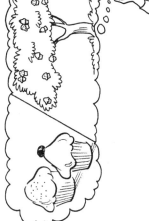

¿Crecen las magdalenas en los árboles?
¡No! Pero si crecieran, eso sería fantástico.

1

Do apples grow on trees?
Yes!

¿Crecen las manzanas en los árboles?
¡Sí!

2

Do cherries grow on trees?
Yes!

¿Crecen las cerezas en los árboles?
¡Sí!

5

Do oranges grow on trees?
Yes!

¿Crecen las naranjas en los árboles?
¡Sí!

6

Do bananas grow on trees?
Yes!

¿Crecen los plátanos en los árboles?
¡Sí!

Clean Up, Clean Up!

¡A recoger, a recoger!

Clean up, clean up!
I put my clothes in the drawer.

¡A recoger, a recoger!
Pongo mi ropa en el cajón.

3

My First Bilingual Little Readers • Level B

© 2007 by Liza Charlesworth, Scholastic Teaching Resources

Clean up, clean up!
I put my shoes in the closet.

¡A recoger, a recoger!
Pongo mis zapatos en el armario.

3

4

"Well done, well done!"
my dad said.

—¡Bien hecho, bien hecho!
—dijo mi papá.

7

2

Clean up, clean up!
I put my books on the shelf.

¡A recoger, a recoger!
Pongo mis libros en el estante.

1

Clean up, clean up!
I put my crayons in the box.

¡A recoger, a recoger!
Pongo mis creyones en la caja.

5

Clean up, clean up!
I put my trash in the can.

¡A recoger, a recoger!
Pongo mi basura en el cesto.

6

Clean up, clean up!
I put my bear on the bed.

¡A recoger, a recoger!
Pongo mi osito en la cama.

A bird flies way up high!

¿Qué vuela?

What Flies?

¡El pájaro vuela muy alto!

My First Bilingual Little Readers • Level B

A kite flies way up high!

but only in my dreams!

¡La cometa vuela muy alto!

¡pero solo en mis sueños!

1

¿Qué vuela en el cielo?

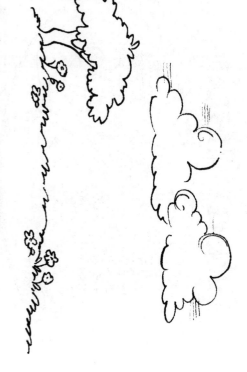

What flies in the sky?

2

¡La abeja vuela muy alto!

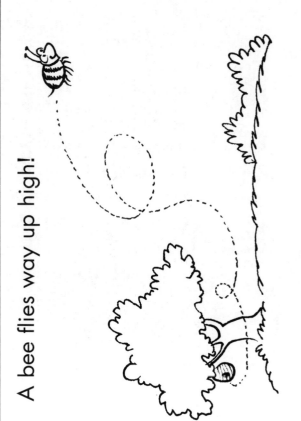

A bee flies way up high!

5

¡El avión vuela muy alto!

A plane flies way up high!

6

Yo vuelo muy alto...

I fly way up high ...

Ella tiene el cabello oscuro.

She has dark hair.

My First Bilingual Little Readers • Level B

© 2007 by Liza Charlesworth, Scholastic Teaching Resources

Great Hair

Hermosos cabellos

Él tiene el cabello claro.

He has light hair.

Everyone has great hair!

¡Todos tienen hermosos cabellos!

1

She has long hair.

Ella tiene el cabello largo.

My First Bilingual Little Readers • Level B

© 2007 by Liza Charlesworth, Scholastic Teaching Resources

2

Él tiene el cabello corto.

He has short hair.

6

El tiene el cabello lacio.

He has straight hair.

5

Ella tiene el cabello rizado.

She has curly hair.

Come Over

Ven a verme

3

Come over and see my lamp.

Ven a ver mi lámpara.

My First Bilingual Little Readers • Level B

© 2007 by Liza Charlesworth, Scholastic Teaching Resources

4

Come over and see my tub.

Ven a ver mi bañera.

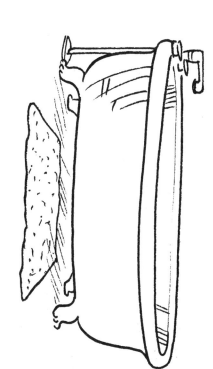

7

Come over and see my dollhouse!

¡Ven a ver mi casa de muñecas!

1

Ven a ver mi silla.

Come over and see my chair.

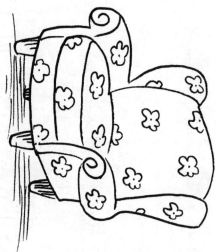

My First Bilingual Little Readers • Level B

© 2007 by Liza Charlesworth, Scholastic Teaching Resources

2

Ven a ver mi mesa.

Come over and see my table.

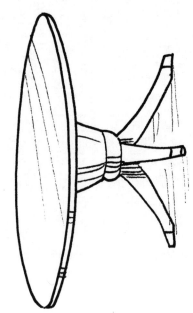

6

Ven a ver mi cómoda.

Come over and see my dresser.

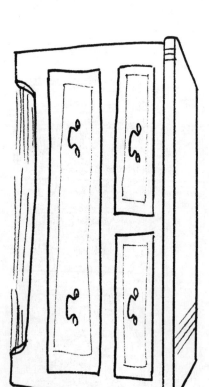

5

Ven a ver mi sofá.

Come over and see my couch.

Aquí está el monstruo.

Here is a monster.

Halloween

My First Bilingual Little Readers • Level B

© 2007 by Liza Charlesworth, Scholastic Teaching Resources

Aquí está la princesa.

Here is a princess.

No, it is just us!
Happy Halloween!

Fiesta de disfraces de la escuela

¡No, somos solo nosotros!
¡Feliz Fiesta de Halloween!

2

Here is an astronaut.

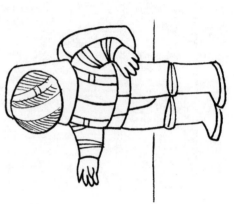

Aquí está el astronauta.

1

Here is a dragon.

Aquí está el dragón.

5

Here is a robot.

Aquí está el robot.

6

Here is a tiger.

Aquí está el tigre.

Party Shapes

Las figuras de la fiesta

Here is a game.
It is a rectangle.

Ponle el rabo al burro

Aquí hay un juego.
Es un rectángulo.

My First Bilingual Little Readers • Level B

© 2007 by Liza Charlesworth, Scholastic Teaching Resources

Here is a present.
It is a square.

Aquí hay un regalo.
Es un cuadrado.

POP!
It was an oval.

¡POP!
Era un óvalo.

1

Come to my party
and see the shapes.

Ven a mi fiesta a ver las figuras.

2

Here is a hat.
It is a triangle.

Aquí hay un sombrero.
Es un triángulo.

6

Here is a balloon.
It is an oval.

Aquí hay un globo.
Es un óvalo.

5

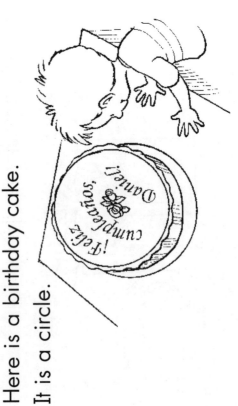

Here is a birthday cake.
It is a circle.

Aquí hay un pastel de cumpleaños.
Es un círculo.

The Missing Monster

El monstruo desaparecido

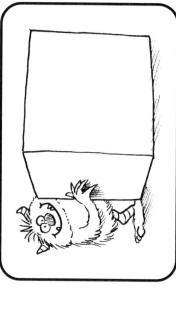

The monster is beside the box.

El monstruo está al lado de la caja.

My First Bilingual Little Readers • Level B

© 2007 by Liza Charlesworth, Scholastic Teaching Resources

The monster is over the box.

El monstruo está por encima de la caja.

The monster is under the box.

El monstruo está debajo de la caja.

2

El monstruo está sobre la caja.

The monster is on the box.

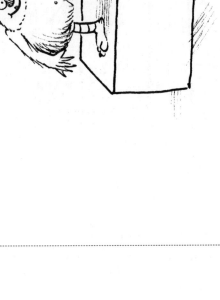

1

El monstruo está en la caja.

The monster is in the box.

¡Oh!

Oh!

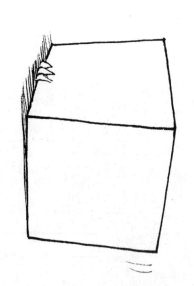

6

Where did the monster go?

¿Adónde se fue el monstruo?

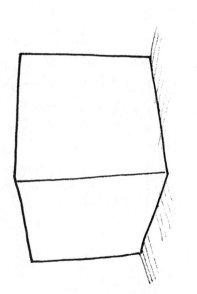

5

The Wheels on the Bus

Las ruedas del autobús

The wheels on the van
go round and round.

Las ruedas de la camioneta
dan vueltas y vueltas.

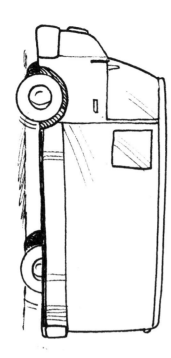

3

The wheels on the motorcycle
go round and round.

Las ruedas de la motocicleta
dan vueltas y vueltas.

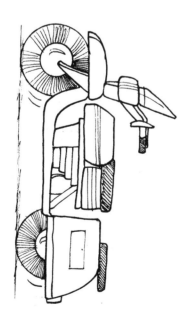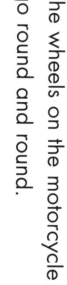

4

The wheels on the vehicles go round
and round, all through my room!

Las ruedas de los vehículos dan vueltas
y vueltas, ¡por toda mi habitación!

7

1

The wheels on the bus
go round and round.

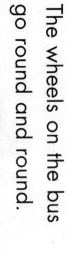

Las ruedas del autobús
dan vueltas y vueltas.

2

The wheels on the car
go round and round.

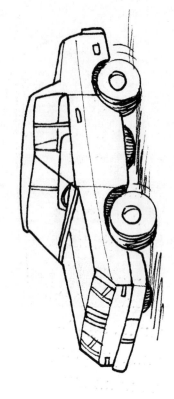

Las ruedas del auto
dan vueltas y vueltas.

My First Bilingual Little Readers • Level B

© 2007 by Liza Charlesworth, Scholastic Teaching Resources

6

The wheels on the fire engine
go round and round.

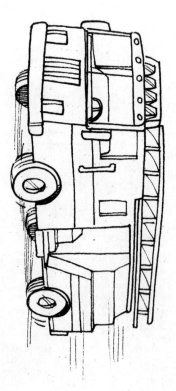

Las ruedas del camión de bomberos
dan vueltas y vueltas.

5

The wheels on the truck
go round and round.

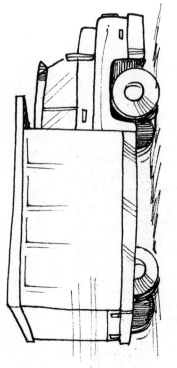

Las ruedas del camión
dan vueltas y vueltas.

I draw 2 squares.
Just like that!

Dibujo 2 cuadrados.
¡Así!

Draw a Cat

Dibuja un gato

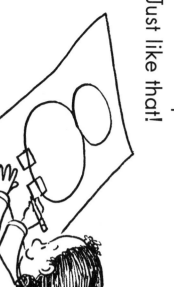

My First Bilingual Little Readers • Level B

© 2007 by Liza Charlesworth, Scholastic Teaching Resources

I draw 3 triangles.
Just like that!

Dibujo 3 triángulos.
¡Así!

I drew a cat.
Just like that!
Now, you try!

Dibujé un gato.
¡Así!
¡Ahora, hazlo tú!

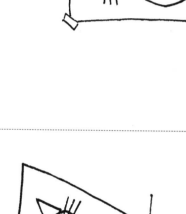

2

I draw 2 circles.
Just like that!

Dibujo 2 círculos.
¡Así!

1

Want to see me draw a cat?

¿Quieres verme dibujar un gato?

5

I draw 2 dots.
Just like that!

Dibujo 2 puntos.
¡Así!

6

I draw 6 lines.
Just like that!

Dibujo 6 líneas.
¡Así!

Bigger

Más grande

The gorilla is bigger than the dog.

El gorila es más grande que el perro.

My First Bilingual Little Readers • Level B

© 2007 by Liza Charlesworth, Scholastic Teaching Resources

The bear is bigger than the gorilla.

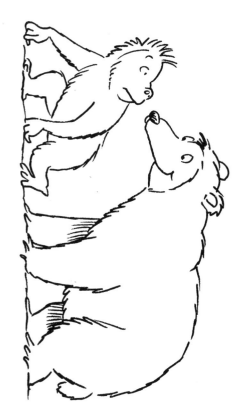

El oso es más grande que el gorila.

But guess what?
The big elephant is afraid of the little mouse!

¿Pero sabes qué?
¡El elefante grande le tiene miedo al ratón pequeño!

2

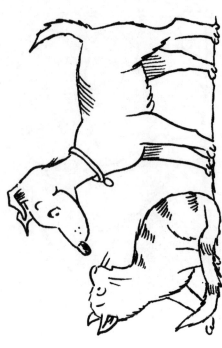

The dog is bigger than the cat.

El perro es más grande que el gato.

1

The cat is bigger than the mouse.

El gato es más grande que el ratón.

5

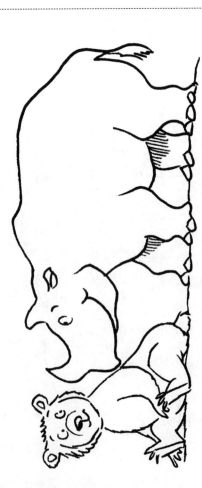

The rhino is bigger than the bear.

El rinoceronte es más grande que el oso.

6

The elephant is bigger than the rhino.

El elefante es más grande que el rinoceronte.

Some monsters eat bugs.

Algunos monstruos comen insectos.

3

What Do Monsters Eat?

¿Qué comen los monstruos?

My First Bilingual Little Readers • Level B

© 2007 by Liza Charlesworth, Scholastic Teaching Resources

Some monsters eat rugs.

Algunos monstruos comen alfombras.

4

What do you like to eat?

¿A ti qué te gusta comer?

7

1

Some monsters eat snakes.

Algunos monstruos comen serpientes.

2

Some monsters eat cakes.

Algunos monstruos comen pasteles.

My First Bilingual Little Readers • Level B

© 2007 by Liza Charlesworth, Scholastic Teaching Resources

6

Some monsters eat socks.

Algunos monstruos comen medias.

5

Some monsters eat rocks.

Algunos monstruos comen rocas.

I have a special shell.

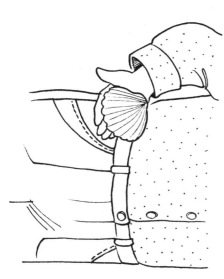

Tengo una caracola especial.

I have a special feather.

Tengo una pluma especial.

In My Pocket

En mi bolsillo

I have a special hamster.
His name is Lenny!

Tengo un hámster especial.
¡Se llama Lenny!

My First Bilingual Little Readers • Level B

© 2007 by Liza Charlesworth, Scholastic Teaching Resources

2

Tengo una piedra especial.

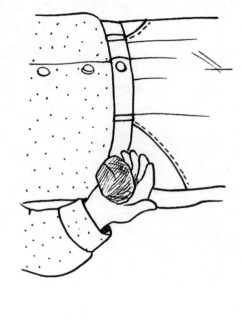

I have a special stone.

1

Do you want to see what I have in my pocket?

¿Quieres ver lo que tengo en mi bolsillo?

5

Tengo una hoja especial.

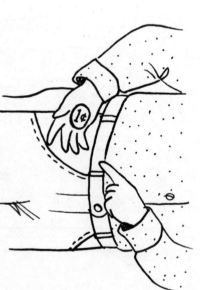

I have a special leaf.

6

I have a special coin.

Tengo una moneda especial.

Look!
This cloud is a bat.

¡Mira!
Esta nube es un murciélago.

Cloud Pictures

Nubes con formas

Look!
This cloud is a flower.

¡Mira!
Esta nube es una flor.

Look!
This cloud is me!

¡Mira!
¡Esta nube soy yo!

1

I like to look up in the sky and see the shapes of the clouds.

Me gusta mirar al cielo y ver las formas de las nubes.

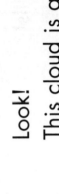

My First Bilingual Little Readers • Level B

2

Look!
This cloud is a hat.

¡Mira!
Esta nube es un sombrero.

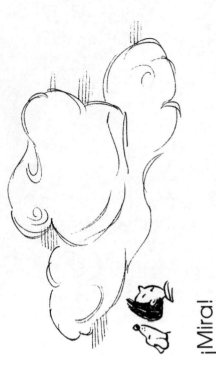

6

Look!
This cloud is a tree.

¡Mira!
Esta nube es un árbol.

5

Look!
This cloud is a tower.

¡Mira!
Esta nube es una torre.

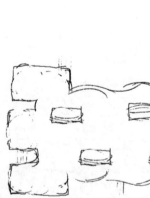

3

I like socks with lots of bells!

¡Me gustan las medias
con muchas campanas!

I Like Socks

Me gustan las medias

I like socks with lots of shells!

¡Me gustan las medias
con muchas caracolas!

4

and so does my cat!

¡y a mi gato también!

7

I like socks with lots of cars!

¡Me gustan las medias con muchos autos!

I like socks with lots of stars!

¡Me gustan las medias con muchas estrellas!

My First Bilingual Little Readers • Level B

© 2007 by Liza Charlesworth, Scholastic Teaching Resources

I like socks with lots of mice...

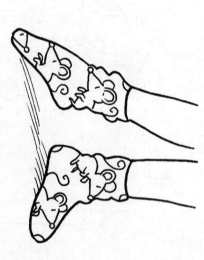

Me gustan las medias con muchos ratones...

I like socks with lots of dice!

¡Me gustan las medias con muchos dados!

Le gusta jugar y jugar.

He likes to play and play.

My First Bilingual Little Readers • Level B

© 2007 by Liza Charlesworth, Scholastic Teaching Resources

Meet My Baby Brother

Te presento a mi hermanito

Le gusta llorar y llorar.

He likes to cry and cry.

It's just too bad he is not so neat!

¡Lástima que no sea muy ordenado!

Meet my baby brother.
His name is Ray.

Te presento a mi hermanito.
Se llama Ray.

He likes to crawl and crawl.

Le gusta gatear y gatear.

My First Bilingual Little Readers • Level B

© 2007 by Liza Charlesworth, Scholastic Teaching Resources

He likes to eat and eat.

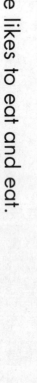

Le gusta comer y comer.

He likes to sleep and sleep.

Le gusta dormir y dormir.